Houghton Mifflin Harcourt School Publishers

Getting Ready for the ISTEP+

Test Preparation and Practice for the Indiana Academic Standards for Mathematics

Use with *HMH Indiana Math* and *Math Expressions*

Includes:

- **Practice Tests in ISTEP+ Format**
- **Content Standards Practice**
- **Vocabulary and Skills Practice**
- **Problem Solving**

Grade 4

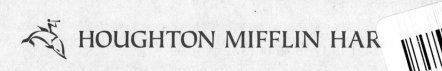

HOUGHTON MIFFLIN HAR

ISBN 13: 978-0-153-86018-8
ISBN 10: 0-153-86018-9

1 2 3 4 5 6 7 8 9 10 1421 18 17 16 15 14 13 12 11 10 09

Contents

Drawing a Picture

Often, it is easier to find a solution to a question if you draw a picture to show the information in the question.

EXAMPLE

Rectangle A and rectangle B share an edge of 12 inches. The shorter side of rectangle A is 6 inches. The length of the longer side of rectangle B is 24 inches. What is the area of rectangle B?

A. 42 in.   **C.** 300 in.

B. 288 in.   **D.** 360 in.

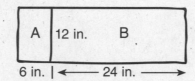

Drawing the rectangles helps you see which numbers to multiply to find the area of rectangle B.

To find the area, multiply the length, 24 inches, by the width, 12 inches: $24 \times 12 = 288$.

So, the correct answer is 288 inches.

Estimating an Answer

You can use estimation to find an answer, check an answer, or eliminate possible answers in multiple-choice questions.

EXAMPLE

Carter goes school-supply shopping. He has only one bill in his wallet and is able to buy one of everything on his list. He receives only coins for his change back.

School Supply List	
Supply	**Cost**
1 pack of pencils	$2.99
1 pack of notebook paper	$1.59
1 spiral notebook	$1.79
1 binder	$2.69

Which bill could Carter have in his wallet?

F. $1   **H.** $10

G. $5   **J.** $20

You can estimate the cost of each item and add the estimated numbers mentally. $2.99 rounds up to $3.00, $1.59 rounds up to $2.00, $1.79 rounds up to $2.00, and $2.69 rounds up to $3.00.

$$\$3 + \$2 + \$2 + \$3 = \$10$$

The first and third answer choices are too low. The fourth answer choice, $20, would allow Carter to buy one of everything; however, he would get bills and coins for change. So, Carter has a $10 bill in his wallet.

Assessment Strategies

Eliminating Answer Choices

You can solve some math problems without doing actual computation. You can use mental math, estimation, or logical reasoning to help you eliminate answer choices and save time.

EXAMPLE

Which number is the closest estimate for 257 + 410?

A. 400

C. 800

B. 700

D. 1,000

You can use logical reasoning to eliminate the first answer choice, 400, because it is too small. The estimated sum has to be greater than 400 because one of the numbers, 410, rounds to 400 and you are adding 257 and 410.

The fourth answer choice, 1,000, can be eliminated because it is too large. The estimated sum will be less than 1,000.

Round 257 up to 300 and 410 down to 400. Then find the sum of 300 and 400: 300 + 400 = 700. You can eliminate the second answer choice because it is greater than 700.

The third answer choice, 700, is the closest estimate.

Answering the Question Asked

EXAMPLE

Deisha's class has a spelling bee each week. She and three other students keep track of how many words they have spelled correctly so far this year. Their results are shown in the table.

Correct Spelling Bee Words	
Name	Number of Words
Deisha	28
Mark	30
Lindsey	18
Roshan	24

Correct Spelling Bee Words	
Name	Number of Words
Deisha	○ ○ ○ ○ ○ ○ ○
Mark	○ ○ ○ ○ ○ ○ ◖
Lindsey	
Roshan	○ ○ ○ ○ ○ ○

Key: Each ○ = 4 words.

How many circles should be shown in the pictograph next to Lindsey's name?

F. $4\frac{1}{2}$

H. 18

G. $7\frac{1}{2}$

J. 24

The question asks for how many circles should go next to Lindsey's name. The second answer choice, 18, shows how many **words** Lindsey spelled correctly, not the number of circles that should be shown next to her name. The third answer choice, $7\frac{1}{2}$, shows how many circles should go next to Mark's name, not Lindsey's name. The last answer choice, 24, is how many words Roshan spelled correctly, not Lindsey. The answer to the question is $4\frac{1}{2}$.

1. **4.1.1** Look at the place-value blocks below.

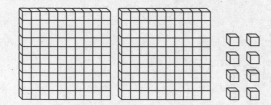

Which number is represented by the place-value blocks?

A. 100

B. 180

C. 208

D. 280

2. **4.2.1** Which value of w correctly solves the equation?

$$w \div 3 = 15$$

F. $w = 5$

G. $w = 12$

H. $w = 18$

J. $w = 45$

3. **4.2.4** Which number sentence demonstrates the distributive property?

A. $(3 \times 8) \times 2 = 3 \times (8 \times 2)$

B. $5 \times 7 = 7 \times 5$.

C. $4(8 + 9) = (4 \times 8) + (4 \times 9)$

D. $6 \times 1 = 6$

Go On ⟹

Getting Ready for the ISTEP+

4. **4.2.4** Madison wants to use the distributive property to solve this expression.

$$30 \times 142$$

Which expression should Madison use?

F. $(30 \times 100) \times (30 \times 40) \times (30 \times 2)$

G. $(30 \times 100) + (30 \times 40) + (30 \times 2)$

H. $(30 + 100) \times (30 + 40) \times (30 + 2)$

J. $(30 + 100) + (30 + 40) + (30 + 2)$

5. **4.1.2** Look at the fraction strips below.

$\frac{1}{6}$	$\frac{1}{6}$	$\frac{1}{6}$	$\frac{1}{6}$	$\frac{1}{6}$	$\frac{1}{6}$

$\frac{1}{4}$	$\frac{1}{4}$	$\frac{1}{4}$	$\frac{1}{4}$

Which answer correctly shows the comparison of the fractions?

A. $\frac{3}{4} < \frac{3}{6}$

B. $\frac{5}{6} > \frac{3}{4}$

C. $\frac{4}{6} < \frac{2}{4}$

D. $\frac{1}{6} > \frac{1}{4}$

6. **4.1.6** Serena collects stamps. She has 34 pages of stamps in her notebook. Each page has 18 stamps. How many stamps does she have in all?

F. 512   H. 632

G. 612   J. 642

Go On

7. ▌4.1.1 Which expression below shows the number 530,967 written in expanded form?

A. 530,000 + 900 + 60 + 7

B. 500,000 + 3,000 + 900 + 60 + 7

C. 530,000 + 900 + 67

D. 500,000 + 30,000 + 900 + 60 + 7

8. ▌4.1.6 The school nurse recorded the following heights in inches of some fourth-grade students.

48　50　51　49　49　50　52　54　61　51　53

What is the median height of the fourth-grade students?

F. 13

G. 50

H. 51

J. 52

9. ▌4.2.3 Which equation is an example of the commutative property of multiplication?

A. 5 × (4 × 5) = 100

B. 72 × 9 = 9 × 72

C. 12 × (3 × 2) = 6 + 66

D. (3 × 3) × 3 = (9 × 3) + 0

Go On ⟹

10. `4.1.3` Which shows the decimal 3.42 written as a mixed number?

    F. $3\frac{42}{100}$

    G. $34\frac{2}{10}$

    H. $3\frac{42}{10}$

    J. $3\frac{42}{50}$

11. `4.1.5` Mike needs 7 pounds of grapes to make one large jar of jelly. He wants to know how many pounds he will need to make 10 jars of jelly.

Which of the following methods can Mike use to multiply 10×7 to solve the problem?

    A. Add 2 zeros to the right of the 7.

    B. Add one zero to the right of the 7.

    C. Write a decimal point before the 7.

    D. Write a decimal point and a 0 before the 7.

12. `4.1.2` Look at the fraction bars below.

$\frac{1}{10}$	$\frac{1}{10}$	$\frac{1}{10}$	$\frac{1}{10}$	$\frac{1}{10}$	$\frac{1}{10}$	$\frac{1}{10}$	$\frac{1}{10}$	$\frac{1}{10}$	$\frac{1}{10}$
$\frac{1}{4}$		$\frac{1}{4}$		$\frac{1}{4}$		$\frac{1}{4}$			

Use the fraction bars to tell which number sentence is true.

    F. $\frac{3}{4} > \frac{7}{10}$ **H.** $\frac{7}{10} > \frac{3}{4}$

    G. $\frac{3}{4} < \frac{7}{10}$ **J.** $\frac{3}{4} = \frac{7}{10}$

Go On ⟶

13. 🔲 4.1.9 Rita placed some cards face down on a table. She picked one card at random. Which describes the likelihood that Rita chose a card with a number that is greater than 8?

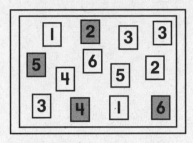

   A. certain   C. unlikely

   B. likely   D. impossible

14. 🔲 4.3.3 The figure below has rotational symmetry.

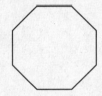

   How many times during one full turn will the figure match its original position?

   F. 2   H. 6

   G. 8   J. 4

15. 🔲 4.3.5 What is the area of this rectangle?

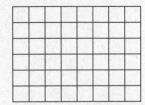

   Area of a rectangle =
   lw = length × width

   A. 14 square units   C. 48 square units

   B. 28 square units   D. 64 square units

Go On ⟶

Getting Ready for the ISTEP+

16 4.1.6 Mrs. Brant's classroom has three bulletin boards—one for math, one for science, and one for reading. Each bulletin board has 24 vocabulary words posted. How many vocabulary words are posted in the classroom?

F. 57

H. 67

G. 62

J. 72

17 4.2.2 Look at the number sequence below.

2, 4, 8, 16, 32, . . .

What is the rule for this pattern?

A. Multiply by 4.

B. Multiply by 2.

C. Add 2.

D. Multiply by 1, then add 2.

18 4.1.3 Use a centimeter ruler as a number line.
Which of these numbers would be located farthest to the right?

F. 3.8

G. 5.2

H. 5.7

J. 5.8

Go On

Getting Ready for the ISTEP+

19 ▌4.2.1 What is the value of *n* in the equation $3n = 20 - 2$?

A. $n = 5p$ **C.** $n = 7p$

B. $n = 6$ **D.** $n = 8$

20 ▌4.1.8 The following graph shows how many miles Calvin hiked at 4 miles per hour.

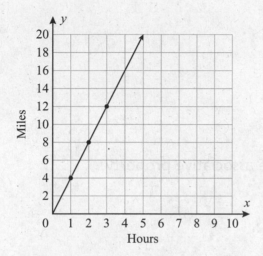

On the graph, what ordered pair will represent the number of miles Calvin hikes after 4 hours?

F. (4, 1)   **H.** (4, 16)

G. (1, 4)   **J.** (16, 4)

21 ▌4.3.2 Which of these angles is an acute angle?

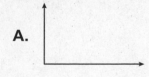

A.   **C.**

B.   **D.**

Go On

22. ▮4.1.3 Which decimal represents the shaded part of the model?

    F. 0.08

    G. 0.80

    H. 0.88

    J. 8.80

23. ▮4.2.3 Which equation shows the associative property of multiplication?

    A. $(9 + 1) \times 3 = (1 + 3) \times 9$

    B. $6 \times 7 = 7 \times 6$

    C. $(9 \times 4) \times 5 = 9 \times (4 \times 5)$

    D. $4(6 + 5) = (4 \times 6) + (4 \times 5)$

24. ▮4.1.4 Which shows nineteen and seven hundredths written as a decimal?

    F. 0.197

    G. 1.907

    H. 19.07

    J. 19.70

Go On ⟹

25. `4.1.9` Ethan is dressing for school. He can wear either a green, orange, or purple shirt. He can wear blue, black, or gray pants. How many different combinations of one shirt and one pair of pants can Ethan make?

A. 25

B. 6

C. 3

D. 9

26. `4.3.5` What is the perimeter of the rectangle below?

3 ft

8 ft

F. 22 cm H. 19 cm

G. 24 cm J. 11 cm

27. `4.1.5` If $p = 8$, what is the value of this expression?

$$(p \times 4) \div 4$$

A. 4

B. 6

C. 8

D. 32

Go On

28. 4.1.4 What decimal number is shown by the shaded part?

    F. 0.07   **H.** 7.0

    G. 0.7   **J.** 70

29. 4.3.2 The flower garden in Mrs. Green's yard is shaped like this triangle.

How many obtuse angles does her garden have?

    A. 0

    B. 1

    C. 2

    D. 3

30. 4.3.3 Which figures have rotational symmetry?

 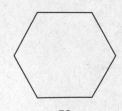 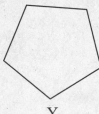 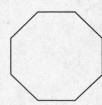

    W   X   Y   Z

    F. W, X, Y   **H.** W, X, Z

    G. X, Y, Z   **J.** W, Y, Z

Go On ⟶

31. `4.3.5` Lynn is making a small box to store beads. The lid of the box will be 12 cm in length and 5 cm in width. Use a centimeter ruler to draw the exact size of the lid. Label the sides.

Lynn wants to decorate the edge of the lid with tiny beads. To do this she needs to know the perimeter of the box lid. Explain how to find the perimeter of the rectangular lid.

_____

Find the perimeter of the lid.

Show All Work

Answer _____ centimeters

Lynn needs to decide whether she has enough beads to completely cover the lid. To do this she must know the area to cover. Find the area of the lid.

Show All Work

Answer _____ square centimeters

Lynn has enough small beads to cover an area of 52 square centimeters. Does she have enough beads? Explain your answer.

_____

_____

Go On

32. **4.1.3** At the Apple Growers Association luncheon, members were seated at four large tables. Each table was served 2 fruit pies for dessert. The members ate different amounts of pie. Here is the amount of pie that was eaten at each table.

Table 1: $1\frac{2}{5}$	Table 3: $1\frac{3}{10}$
Table 2: 1.8	Table 4: $1\frac{3}{4}$

What is the total amount of pie eaten by all the tables in decimal form?

Show All Work

Answer _____ pies

What is that number as a fraction?

Answer _____ pies

How much pie was left? Show that number as a fraction.

Answer _____ pies

STOP

1. **4.1.1** Which answer below shows the number 706 written using words?

   A. seventy-six

   B. seven hundred six

   C. seven hundred sixty

   D. seventy-six hundred

2. **4.2.2** Look at the number sequence below.

   6, 12, 24, 48 196, . . .

   What is the rule for this pattern?

   F. add 4

   G. multiply by 2

   H. multiply by 4

   J. multiply by 1, then add 6

3. **4.2.4** Which number sentence shows the correct method of applying the distributive property to the formula for the perimeter of a rectangle?

   A. $p = 2(l + w) = 2l + 2w$

   B. $p = 2(l + w) = 2 + l + w$

   C. $p = 2(l \times w) = 2l \times 2w$

   D. $p = 2(l \times w) = 2 + l + 2 + w$

Go On

Name _____

4. **4.1.4** Which of the following decimal numbers is represented by the model below?

F. 0.16

G. 0.17

H. 0.18

J. 0.27

5. **4.1.7** The large rectangle below represents one whole. If 3 of the small squares are removed, what fraction of the rectangle remains?

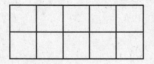

A. $\frac{3}{10}$

B. $\frac{7}{10}$

C. $\frac{7}{7}$

D. $\frac{13}{10}$

6. ▮**4.2.4** Andrew wants to use the distributive property to solve this expression.

$$80 \times 137$$

Which expression should Andrew use?

F. $(80 \times 100) \times (80 \times 30) \times (80 \times 7)$

G. $(80 \times 100) + (80 + 30) + (80 \times 7)$

H. $(80 \times 100) \times (80 + 30) + (80 \times 7)$

J. $(80 \times 100) + (80 \times 30) + (80 \times 7)$

7. ▮**4.1.2** Look at the fraction models below.

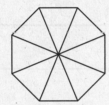 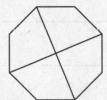

Which number sentence correctly compares the fractions?

A. $\frac{3}{4} < \frac{3}{8}$

B. $\frac{1}{8} > \frac{1}{4}$

C. $\frac{2}{4} = \frac{4}{8}$

D. $\frac{7}{8} < \frac{3}{4}$

Go On

8. **4.3.1** The population of Indianapolis is 795,068.

Write the population of Indianapolis in expanded form.

Answer _____

Explain how you found the value of each digit.

_____

_____

_____

_____

_____

_____

_____

_____

Write the population of Indianapolis in word form.

Answer _____

_____

9. **4.1.4** What decimal is represented by the model?

F. 0.02   **H.** 22.0

G. 0.22   **J.** 202

Go On ▷

Name _____

10. `4.3.3` Which of these figures has rotational symmetry?

A.

C.

B.

D.

11. `4.1.6` Look at the data below.

24, 28, 25, 29, 25, 30, 26

What is the mode of this set of data?

F. 6   H. 26

G. 25   J. 27

12. `4.3.2` Which of the triangles below contains a right angle?

A.

C.

B.

D.

13. `4.1.5` If $m = 8$, what is the value of the expression?

$$m \times 5 = \underline{\hspace{2cm}}$$

F. 32   H. 48

G. 40   J. 50

Go On ⟶

Getting Ready for the ISTEP+

14. **4.1.7** Look at the models of the fractions below.

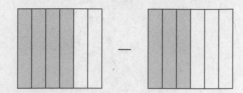

Which is the fraction subtraction sentence represented by the models?

A. $\frac{4}{6} - \frac{3}{6}$ C. $\frac{4}{6} + \frac{2}{6} - \frac{3}{6}$

B. $\frac{2}{6} - \frac{3}{6}$ D. $1 - \frac{3}{6}$

15. **4.2.3** Which equation is an example of the commutative property of multiplication?

F. $6 \times 19 = 19 \times 6$ H. $2 \times (5 \times 4) = 15 + 25$

G. $3 \times (4 \times 2) = 30 - 6$ J. $(6 \times 9) \times 1 = 54$

16. **4.1.3** Which decimal measure on the centimeter ruler is shown by the arrow?

A. 4.1 centimeters   C. 4.5 centimeters

B. 4.3 centimeters   D. 4.6 centimeters

17. **4.1.6** A box contains 24 ginger cookies. Each cookie contains 44 calories. Paul's dog ate an entire box of ginger cookies. How many calories did the dog eat?

F. 1,036   H. 1,056

G. 1,046   J. 1,066

Name _____

18. **4.1.9** Emma puts 12 marbles in a bag. There are 4 blue marbles and 8 white marbles. Emma reaches into the bag and removes a marble. Which shows the probability that the marble will be white?

A. $\frac{4}{8}$ C. $\frac{20}{12}$

B. $\frac{8}{12}$ D. $\frac{4}{12}$

19. **4.1.4** In the number 87.63, which digit is in the hundredths place?

F. 8

G. 7

H. 6

J. 3

20. **4.3.5** Darcy wants to cover her bedroom floor with carpet. The diagram below shows her bedroom.

Which expression could she use to find the amount of carpet she needs to cover the floor of her bedroom?

A. 12 × 10   C. 12 + 12 + 10 + 10

B. 12 + 10   D. 12 × 12 × 10 × 10

Go On

21. (4.1.5) Which expression shows the dollar amount $3.82 written in expanded form?

F. $3.00 + $0.80 + $0.02

G. $3 + $8 + $2

H. $30.00 + $8.00 + $0.20

J. $300 + $80 + $20

22. (4.1.3) Which of the angles below appears to be a right angle?

A.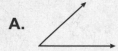

B.

C.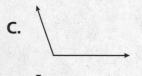

D.

23. (4.1.5) The girls' field hockey team has 24 members. One-quarter of the team members scored a goal last week.

Which number sentence should you use to find out how many team members scored a goal last week?

F. $24 \div 4 = 6$

G. $24 \times 4 = 96$

H. $24 \times 6 = 144$

J. $24 \div 3 = 8$

Go On

24. ◗ 4.2.1 Tyrone can run 15 miles in 3 hours. Which equation can be used to find how far he can run in 1 hour?

A. $15 - 3 = m$

B. $3m = 15$

C. $15 + 3 = m$

D. $15m = 3$

25. ◗ 4.3.1 Look at the quadrilateral below.

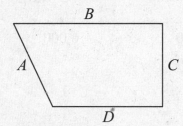

Which sides of the quadrilateral seem to be made of parallel line segments?

F. *A* and *B*   H. *B* and *C*

G. *A* and *C*   J. *B* and *D*

26. ◗ 4.1.9 The Rockets team members have a choice of uniform. The uniform is either a blue or a white shirt, and either red, white or blue shorts. How many different combinations can a Rocket player wear?

A. 2

B. 3

C. 5

D. 6

Go On ⇨

27. **4.1.4** What is $\frac{8}{100}$ written as a decimal?

    F. 0.80

    G. 0.08

    H. 8.08

    J. 880.00

28. **4.1.1** What number does the point at x represent on the number line?

    A. 5488

    B. 5982

    C. 5693

    D. 5272

29. **4.2.1** What is the value of n in the equation $4n = 17 + 3$?

    F. 5

    G. 4

    H. 3

    J. 20

Go On

30. ▌ **4.3.5** The town of Greenville is putting a new lawn in their park. The drawing shows the land where the grass will be planted. What is the area that the grass seed must cover?

Show All Work

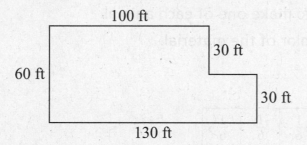

Answer _____ square feet

Jake's job is to buy the grass seed. Each bag of seed covers 1,000 square feet.

How many bags of seed will Jake need to buy?

Answer _____ bags of seed

Go On ⟶

31. **4.1.2** Marla is helping to make small stuffed animals for a school fundraiser. She needs $\frac{5}{6}$ yards of brown material to make a teddy bear. She needs $\frac{7}{8}$ yards of grey material for an elephant. Shade the fraction bars below to show how much material Marla needs in order to make one of each animal. Label the bars to identify the color of the material.

Show All Work

$\frac{1}{6}$	$\frac{1}{6}$	$\frac{1}{6}$	$\frac{1}{6}$	$\frac{1}{6}$	$\frac{1}{6}$

$\frac{1}{8}$	$\frac{1}{8}$	$\frac{1}{8}$	$\frac{1}{8}$	$\frac{1}{8}$	$\frac{1}{8}$	$\frac{1}{8}$	$\frac{1}{8}$

Which color material does Carla need more of? How much more does she need of that color?

Answer: _____

Write a comparison that shows how the lengths compare.

Answer _____

STOP

1. **4.1.1** Becca was asked to round 482,208 to the nearest hundred thousand. The number 482,208 is between which of the following numbers?

   A. 480,000 and 490,000

   B. 482,000 and 483,000

   C. 400,000 and 500,000

   D. 4,000,000 and 5,000,000

2. **4.2.2** Write the number nineteen and four hundredths as a decimal.

   _____

3. **4.2.5** What is the area of the rectangle shown below?

   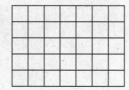

   Area of a rectangle =
   lw = length × width

   A. 12 square units

   B. 30 square units

   C. 35 square units

   D. 49 square units

Go On ⟹

4. ▮4.1.3 Which answer below shows the decimal number 5.3 written as a mixed number?

   F. $3\frac{5}{10}$

   G. $3\frac{5}{100}$

   H. $5\frac{3}{100}$

   J. $5\frac{3}{10}$

5. ▮4.2.1 What is the missing factor in the equation $4 \times m = 24$?

   A. $m = 3$

   B. $m = 4$

   C. $m = 5$

   D. $m = 6$

6. ▮4.2.2 Look at the number sequence below.

   2, 5, 11, 23, 47, . . .

   What is the rule for this pattern?

   F. add 4

   G. multiply by 6

   H. multiply by 3

   J. multiply by 2, then add 1

Go On

7. **4.1.8** Jack took a survey of favorite colors. He asked each student in the class to choose from four colors. He recorded the results in a frequency table.

Favorite Color

Color	red	blue	green	yellow
Frequency	9	11	4	5

How many students did he survey in all?

A. 25

B. 27

C. 29

D. 31

8. **4.2.3** Which equation is an example of the associative property of multiplication?

F. $4 + (7 \times 3) = (20 + 5)$

G. $(18 \times 6) \times 2 = 18 \times (6 \times 2)$

H. $3 \times 2 = 2 \times 3$

J. $(4 \times 8) \times 2 = 64$

9. **4.2.3** What is $\frac{13}{100}$ written as a decimal?

A. 0.013

B.   0.13

C. 1.13

D. 13.10

Go On

10. 📘 4.1.2 Which comparison is true? Use the fraction models below.

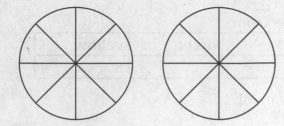

F. $\frac{3}{8} > \frac{7}{8}$

G. $\frac{7}{8} > \frac{5}{8}$

H. $\frac{3}{8} = \frac{5}{8}$

J. $\frac{5}{8} < \frac{3}{8}$

11. 📘 4.3.1 Look at the diagram below.

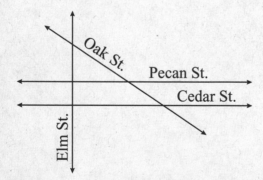

Which pair of streets do NOT intersect?

A. Cedar St. and Elm St.

B. Oak St. and Elm St.

C. Pecan St. and Cedar St.

D. Pecan St. and Elm St.

Go On ⟹

Practice C

28

Getting Ready for the ISTEP+

12. ▋4.2.4 Which number sentence demonstrates the distributive property?

A. $7 \times 2 = 14$

B. $(4 \times 6) \times 3 = 4 \times (6 \times 3)$

C. $9 \times 3 = 3 \times 9$

D. $5(7 + 8) = (5 \times 7) + (5 \times 8)$

13. ▋4.1.6 Dee made a fancy collar for each of her 4 dogs. She sewed 23 beads on each collar. How many beads did she sew on all the collars?

F. 27

G. 46

H. 69

J. 92

14. ▋4.3.3 Which three letters all have rotational symmetry?

A. T, O, N

B. C, O, E

C. T, L, Z

D. H, S, Z

Go On ⇒

15. ▮4.1.6 Renee has art class for 60 minutes each week of the school year. There are 36 weeks of school. For how many minutes does she have art class during the school year?

    F. 216 minutes

    G. 266 minutes

    H. 2,160 minutes

    J. 2,660 minutes

16. ▮4.3.2 Which of the angles below appears to be an acute angle?

A.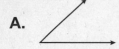

B.

C.

D.

17. ▮4.1.5 Look at the spinner below.

What is the probability the spinner will stop in Sector B?

    F. $\frac{1}{8}$ **H.** $\frac{3}{8}$

    G. $\frac{2}{8}$ **J.** $\frac{8}{8}$

Go On ⟹

18. 🔖 **4.1.7** The model below represents one whole. If 4 of the sections are removed, what fraction of the model remains?

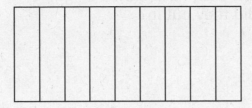

A. $\frac{4}{9}$

B. $\frac{5}{9}$

C. $\frac{9}{9}$

D. $\frac{13}{9}$

19. 🔖 **4.2.3** Which equation is an example of the commutative property of multiplication?

F. $2 \times (5 \times 4) = 15 + 25$

G. $3 \times (5 \times 5) = 100 - 25$

H. $7 \times 4 = 4 \times 7$

J. $(5 \times 3) \times 5 = 75$

20. 🔖 **4.1.3** Which answer below shows the decimal number 5.4 written as a mixed number?

A. $\frac{54}{100}$

B. $5\frac{4}{100}$

C. $5\frac{4}{10}$

D. $\frac{5}{10}$

Go On ⟶

Getting Ready for the ISTEP+

21. 4.1.5 When they moved into their new home, the Marinos put new light bulbs in all the fixtures. The new house had 6 rooms, and each room had 3 fixtures. Each fixture used 2 light bulbs. How many new light bulbs did they put in?

F. 6

G. 12

H. 18

J. 36

22. 4.1.2 Look at the fraction bars below.

$\frac{1}{6}$	$\frac{1}{6}$	$\frac{1}{6}$	$\frac{1}{6}$	$\frac{1}{6}$	$\frac{1}{6}$

$\frac{1}{8}$	$\frac{1}{8}$	$\frac{1}{8}$	$\frac{1}{8}$	$\frac{1}{8}$	$\frac{1}{8}$	$\frac{1}{8}$	$\frac{1}{8}$

Use the fraction bars to tell which number sentence is true.

A. $\frac{3}{6} > \frac{4}{8}$

B. $\frac{4}{8} > \frac{3}{6}$

C. $\frac{4}{8} = \frac{3}{6}$

D. $\frac{3}{6} < \frac{4}{8}$

23. 4.1.9 Logan and Jacob made sandwiches for school visitors. They had white bread, rye bread, and whole wheat bread. They could make tuna fish, cheese, or peanut butter sandwiches. How many possible combinations of sandwiches can they make using one kind of bread and one filling for each sandwich?

F. 6

G. 8

H. 9

J. 12

Go On ⟹

24. `4.3.4` Use a centimeter ruler to measure the length of the marker. What is the length?

F. $\frac{3}{12}$ cm   H. 9 cm

G. 8 cm   J. 10 cm

25. `4.1.9` Ava rolls a number cube that is labeled 1 to 6. What is the probability that the cube will land on a number less than 4?

F. $\frac{1}{6}$

G. $\frac{2}{6}$

H. $\frac{1}{4}$

J. $\frac{3}{6}$

26. `4.1.4` Which number shows eleven and fourteen hundredths?

A. 111.4

B. 1114

C. 11.14

D. 11.141

27. `4.1.5` What is the fourth multiple of 2?

   F. 6

   G. 7

   H. 8

   J. 9

28. `4.2.4` Find the missing number using the distributive property.

$$47 \times 63 = (47 \times \square) + (47 \times 3)$$

   A. 47

   B. 63

   C. 40

   D. 60

29. `4.3.2` Todd printed 90 pages of pictures. There were 8 small pictures on each page. Todd cut out the pictures and arranged them in groups of 6 to make books for young children. If he used all of the pictures, how many books did he make?

   F. 120

   G. 130

   H. 140

   J. 150

Go On

Getting Ready for the ISTEP+

30. ▌4.1.1▐ Look at the place-value blocks shown below.

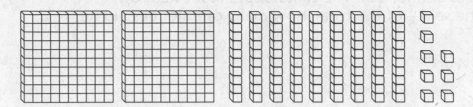

What number is shown?

Answer: _____

Look at the additional place-value blocks.

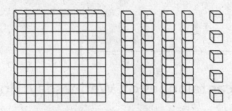

Show All Work

If these place value blocks are included with the previous model, what new number will be shown?

Answer: _____

Suppose that instead of including these place value blocks, their value was subtracted from the previous model. What new number would be shown then?

Answer: _____

Go On ▷

32. ▮ 4.1.3 Mr. Gordon's grocery received a shipment of 160 cantaloupes on Monday. The cantaloupes cost $1.25. On Monday he sold $\frac{1}{5}$ of the total. How many cantaloupes did he sell?

Show All Work

Answer:_____

How much money was paid?

Answer: _____

He sold another $\frac{3}{4}$ of the cantaloupes on Wednesday. How many cantaloupes were sold and what was the total paid on Wednesday?

Answer: _____

Core Standard 1 Number Sense and Computation

■ 4.1.1 **Count, read, write, compare and plot whole numbers using words, models, number lines and expanded form.**

1. What is the standard form for $70,000 + 2,000 + 500 + 7$?

   A. 7,257

   B. 72,057

   C. 72,507

   D. 702,507

2. What is sixty-four thousand, one hundred twenty-six in standard form?

   F. 64,016

   G. 64,026

   H. 64,106

   J. 64,126

3. This year, Ann rode 3,100 miles on her bicycle. Tom rode 3,025 miles. Amy rode 3,250 miles.

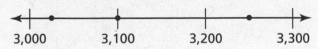

Which shows the distances they rode ordered from greatest to least?

   A. 3,025   3,100   3,250

   B. 3,100   3,025   3,250

   C. 3,250   3,025   3,100

   D. 3,250   3,100   3,025

4. Which number completes the number sentence?

   $$26,720 = 20,000 + 6,000 + 700 + \square$$

   F. 2

   G. 20

   H. 200

   J. 2,000

5. The school librarian makes a new rule to limit the number of books each student can check out at one time. She writes an inequality to show how many books, b, each student can check out at one time.

   $$b < 12$$

   Dianne chooses 15 books that she would like to check out. She plots this number of books on the number line.

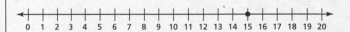

   Dianne realizes that she has taken too many books, but she wants to keep as many books as possible.

   How many books will Dianne have to put back?

   A. 1   C. 3

   B. 2   D. 4

Getting Ready for the ISTEP+

6. Sandra writes a number on the board.

34,920

Write the number in word form.

_____

_____

7. Two hundred forty-three thousand, six hundred sixty-one people attended the country fair in the month of August

Thousands			Ones		
Hundreds	Tens	Ones	Hundreds	Tens	Ones
2	■	3	6	6	1

Write the number that completes the place-value chart.

_____

Core Standard 1 Number Sense and Computation

4.1.2 Find equivalent fractions and then use them to compare and order whole numbers and fractions using the symbols for less than (<), equals (=), and greater than (>).

1. Mark made this model.

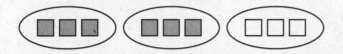

   Which shows an equivalent fraction for $\frac{6}{9}$?

   A. $\frac{2}{3}$

   B. $\frac{4}{9}$

   C. $\frac{1}{3}$

   D. $\frac{2}{9}$

2. Which lists the fractions in order from *least* to *greatest*?

   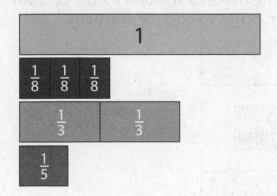

   F. $\frac{1}{5}, \frac{3}{8}, \frac{2}{3}$

   G. $\frac{1}{5}, \frac{2}{3}, \frac{3}{8}$

   H. $\frac{3}{8}, \frac{2}{3}, \frac{1}{5}$

   J. $\frac{2}{3}, \frac{3}{8}, \frac{1}{5}$

3. Jaime wants to write a fraction that is closer to 1 than $\frac{4}{6}$. Which fraction could she write?

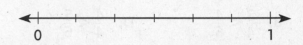

   A. $\frac{5}{6}$ C. $\frac{1}{6}$

   B. $\frac{3}{6}$ D. $\frac{2}{6}$

4. Ben ate $\frac{5}{12}$ pound of popcorn, Allen ate $\frac{5}{6}$ pound, and Brandon ate $\frac{7}{12}$ pound. Which shows the amounts of popcorn they ate in order from greatest to least?

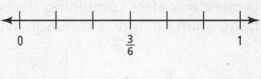

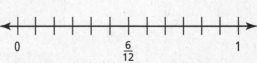

   F. $\frac{5}{12}, \frac{5}{6}, \frac{7}{12}$

   G. $\frac{5}{12}, \frac{7}{12}, \frac{5}{6}$

   H. $\frac{5}{6}, \frac{5}{12}, \frac{7}{12}$

   J. $\frac{5}{6}, \frac{7}{12}, \frac{5}{12}$

6. Use the fraction bars to tell which number sentence is true.

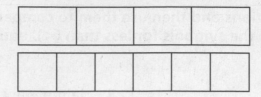

A. $\frac{2}{4} = \frac{3}{6}$

C. $\frac{1}{4} > \frac{2}{6}$

B. $\frac{3}{4} < \frac{4}{6}$

D. $\frac{4}{4} < \frac{5}{6}$

7. Aaron wrote two fractions. Compare the fractions using <, >, or =.

$$\frac{1}{8} \bigcirc \frac{1}{2}$$

_____

8. Jeremy is helping his mother build a swing set in their backyard. They need enough cement to set the poles for the swing set in the ground. Jeremy finds two bags of cement. One bag has $\frac{2}{5}$ kilogram of cement mix. The other bag has $\frac{3}{10}$ kilogram of cement mix.

Jeremy combines the 2 bags of cement mix. He wants to know the weight of the cement mix after combining the two bags, so he makes a fraction model of both bags. Then he finds a common denominator in order to add the fractions.

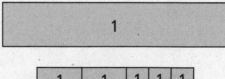

Look at Jeremy's fraction models. What is the weight of the cement mix after Jeremy combines the 2 bags?

A. $\frac{1}{10}$ kilogram

C. $\frac{7}{10}$ kilogram

B. $\frac{4}{10}$ kilogram

D. $\frac{4}{5}$ kilogram

Core Standard 1 Number Sense and Computation

4.1.3 Solve problems involving decimals to hundredths.

1. Geraldine has completed $\frac{8}{10}$ of her oral presentation.

What decimal is shown by the shaded part of the model?

A. 0.08   C. 0.4

B. 0.2   D. 0.8

2. Andy threw a paper airplane 5.6 meters.

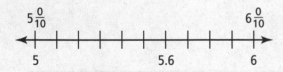

Which mixed number is equivalent to 5.6?

F. $5\frac{1}{10}$

G. $5\frac{5}{10}$

H. $5\frac{6}{10}$

J. $5\frac{5}{6}$

3. John spent $2\frac{2}{10}$ hours practicing for his dance recital.

Which shows $2\frac{2}{10}$ written as a decimal?

A. 0.02   C. 2.02

B. 0.2   D. 2.2

4. Serena used 0.13 pound of cedar chips to line her hamster's cage.

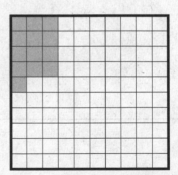

What fraction is shown by the shaded part of the model?

F. $\frac{3}{100}$ H. $\frac{1}{3}$

G. $\frac{13}{100}$ J. $\frac{13}{10}$

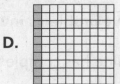

6. Which array model shows 0.4?

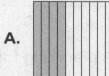 **A.**   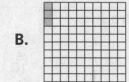 **B.**   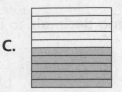 **C.**   **D.**

7. Name the shaded part of the array model as a decimal number.

_____

8. Which of these numbers cannot be placed on the number line shown? Explain.

1.6 1.8 2.1 0.8 2.2

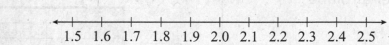

_____

_____

Core Standard 1 Number Sense and Computation

4.1.4 **Use words, models, standard form and expanded form to represent place value of decimal numbers to hundredths.**

1. Which has the numbers ordered from least to greatest?

   A. 0.19, 0.91, 1.09, 1.90

   B. 0.91, 0.19, 1.09. 1.90

   C. 1.90, 1.09, 0.91, 0.19

   D. 1.09, 1.90, 0.19, 0.91

2. What decimal number is represented by the shaded portion of the model?

   F. 0.30

   G. 0.97

   H. 9.70

   J. 97.0

3. Write 17/100 as a decimal.

   _____

4. What is 4.187 written in expanded form?

   F. .40 + 0.18 + 0.07

   G. 4 + 0.1 + 0.08 + 0.007

   H. 04 + 1.0 + 0.08 + 0.7

   J. 40 + 1 + 0.8 + 0.07

5. In the number 123.05, what number is in the tenths place?

   A. 3

   B. 2

   C. 0

   D. 5

6. What is one hundred fifteen and fifteen hundredths in standard form?

   F. 115.115

   G. 100.15

   H. 1500.15

   J. 115.15

7. Write three and seventh hundredths as a decimal in standard form.

_____

8. Which is greater, 0.09 or 0.1? Explain.

_____

_____

_____

_____

Core Standard 1 Number Sense and Computation

4.1.5 Demonstrate fluency with multiplication facts for numbers up to at least 10 and the related division facts. Identify factors of whole numbers and multiplies of whole numbers to 10.

1. Which shows all the factors of 32?

   A. 1, 32

   B. 1, 2, 4, 8, 16, 32

   C. 1, 2, 16, 32

   D. 1, 2, 3, 4, 6, 8, 16, 32

2. Which shows all the factors of 6?

   F. 6, 12, 18, 24

   G. 2, 3, 6

   H. 1, 2, 3, 6

   J. 2, 3

3. Which number makes the sentence *true*?

   All multiples of 8 are also multiples of □.

   A. 2

   B. 6

   C. 18

   D. 24

4. Becka wants to learn about division patterns. What is the pattern for the ones digits of multiples of 6?

   F. 0, 1, 2, 3, 6

   G. 6, 2, 8, 4, 0

   H. 6, 12, 18, 24

   J. 12, 24, 48, 96

5. Josh needs to put 72 bowling balls onto racks. He can fit 8 bowling balls on each rack. Which shows the number of racks Josh will need?

   A. 8

   B. 9

   C. 10

   D. 11

6. Mr. Buckley is counting his coins. He stacks the coins in 7 piles of 12 coins each. How many coins does Mr. Buckley have?

   A. 20   B. 25

   C. 84   D. 840

Name _____

7. Daniel and his family are planning to hike a 42-mile trail. They will hike an equal distance each day for 7 days. How many miles will Daniel and his family hike each day?

_____

8. Anna writes the fact family for the numbers 4, 5, and 20.

$4 \times 5 = 20$ $20 \div \square = 5$

$5 \times 4 = 20$ $20 \div 5 = 4$

What is the missing number?

_____

Core Standard 1 Number Sense and Computation

4.1.6 Solve problems using multiplication of two-digit by single-digit and two-digit numbers fluently using a standard algorithmic approach.

1. Trent is making copies of a 10-page short story. How many pieces of paper will he need to make 20 copies of the story?

   A. 20   C. 200

   B. 100   D. 2,000

2. Maria is planning a spaghetti dinner for 34 guests. She needs to cook 4 ounces of spaghetti for each guest. How many ounces of spaghetti will Maria need to feed all of her guests?

   F. 38 ounces

   G. 126 ounces

   H. 136 ounces

   J. 140 ounces

3. The 15 students in Anna's book group each take turns reading aloud from a novel. Each student reads aloud for 30 minutes. Which shows the total number of minutes the students will read aloud?

   A. 40 minutes

   B. 45 minutes

   C. 400 minutes

   D. 450 minutes

4. Benjamin is training for a triathlon. He is planning to ride his bicycle 18 kilometers a day for 63 days. What is the total distance Benjamin will ride his bicycle?

   F. 1,034 kilometers

   G. 1,114 kilometers

   H. 1,134 kilometers

   J. 1,234 kilometers

5. Kevin's class is selling stuffed animals after school to raise money for wildlife conservation. They have 200 stuffed animals that sell for $8 each. Which equation shows a basic fact Kevin could use to help him find the total amount of money his class will make if all the stuffed animals are sold?

   A. $2 + 8 = 10$

   B. $2 \times 8 = 16$

   C. $8 - 2 = 6$

   D. $8 \div 2 = 4$

Getting Ready for the ISTEP+

6. At the school carnival, tickets can be exchanged for prizes. Mason wants a comic book that costs 160 tickets. If he earns 8 tickets for each game of skee ball, how many games will he need to play to collect enough tickets for the comic book?

F. 18

G. 19

H. 20

J. 21

7. A math book costs $37. Mrs. Jordan's class needs 24 books. What expression will give Mrs. Jordan the most reasonable estimate of the cost of books for her class? What is the total cost of the books?

_____

_____

8. Diane and Adam are reading the same book. Diane has read 24 pages a day for 12 days. Adam has read 32 pages a day for 7 days. How many more pages has Diane read than Adam?

_____

Core Standard 1 Number Sense and Computation

▌4.1.7 Model addition and subtraction of simple fractions.

1. Aisha has $3\frac{2}{9}$ cups of flour and uses $\frac{4}{9}$ cup. How much flour does Aisha have left?

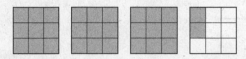

  A. $2\frac{7}{9}$

  B. $2\frac{8}{9}$

  C. $2\frac{11}{9}$

  D. $3\frac{6}{9}$

2. The large rectangle represents one whole. If the shaded squares are removed, what fraction of the large rectangle remains?

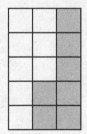

  F. $\frac{7}{15}$

  G. $\frac{1}{2}$

  H. $\frac{2}{3}$

  J. $\frac{8}{15}$

3. Jodi has to read $\frac{7}{8}$ of a book by Thursday. She has already read $\frac{4}{8}$ of the book. Which shows the fraction of the book Jodi has left to read?

  A. $\frac{1}{8}$ **C.** $\frac{3}{8}$

  B. $\frac{2}{12}$ **D.** $\frac{11}{8}$

4. The large rectangle represents one whole. If 1 more small square is added to the rectangle, what mixed number will the figure represent?

  F. $1\frac{1}{2}$ **H.** $2\frac{1}{2}$

  G. $1\frac{1}{6}$ **J.** $2\frac{1}{6}$

5. Use the fraction bar to find the sum $\frac{3}{8} + \frac{3}{8}$.

  A. $\frac{2}{8}$ **C.** $\frac{6}{8}$

  B. $\frac{3}{8}$ **D.** $\frac{8}{8}$

Getting Ready for the ISTEP+

6. Find the sum.

$$\frac{11}{16} + \frac{5}{16} = $$ _____

7. Find the difference.

$$\frac{7}{9} - \frac{2}{9} = $$ _____

8. Look at the fraction models.

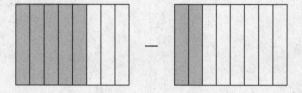

Write a subtraction sentence represented by the models and find the difference.

_____ – _____ = _____

4.1.8 Construct and analyze line plots. Given a set of data or a graph, describe the distribution of the data using median, range or mode.

1. The line plot shows the shoe sizes of all the students in one classroom. What is the range of shoe sizes?

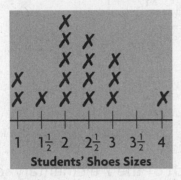

Students' Shoes Sizes

A. 1   C. 3

B. 2   D. 4

2. Amber asked 20 boys and 20 girls what kind of cookies they like best. She recorded her results in this table.

Favorite Cookies		
Cookie	Boys	Girls
Chocolate Chip	12	6
Oatmeal	3	5
Sugar	5	9

What kind of graph would be the best way for Amber to show her data?

F. bar graph

G. double bar graph

H. pictograph

J. line graph

3. The table shows the number of cars a salesperson sells each month.

Casey's Car Sales					
Month	Jan	Feb	Mar	Apr	May
Cars	2	5	1	7	5

What is the mean number of cars she sells?

A. 4   C. 6

B. 5   D. 7

4. This frequency table shows the low temperature in Don's town for the 18 coldest days in January.

Coldest Days in January					
Temperature (°F)	5	10	12	13	15
Frequency	4	5	6	2	1

What is the median temperature for those 18 days?

F. 10   H. 12

G. 11   J. 13

5. Matthew kept track of the number of phone calls he made each week for 7 weeks.

    23, 18, 15, 19, 23, 23, 19

What is the mode of the data set?

A. 15   C. 19

B. 18   D. 23

Name _____

6. Martha asked customers at an ice-cream parlor what their favorite flavors are. She recorded her results in frequency table.

Favorite Ice Cream Flavor				
Flavor	Chocolate	Vanilla	Strawberry	Mint Chip
Frequency	6	8	4	12

How many people did she survey in all?

_____

7. Terrence wrote down the number of students in each of the 7 elementary schools in his city.

729, 925, 620, 620, 645, 728, 984

What is the median of this set of data?

_____

8. Ginny asked her friends how many television shows they watched last night. Their answers were: 1, 2, 3, 5, 2, 2, 4, 0, 1. Find the range, median, and mode of the data set.

range _____

median _____

mode _____

4.1.9 **List all the possible outcomes of a given situation or event. Represent the probability of a given outcome using a picture or other graphic.**

1. Troy set some cards face down and picked one at random. Which describes the likelihood that Troy chose a card with a number that is less than 10?

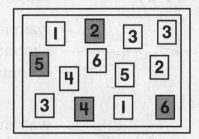

   A. certain   C. unlikely

   B. likely   D. impossible

2. Tanya rolls a number cube labeled 1 to 6. What is the probability that the cube will land on a number less than 3?

   F. $\frac{1}{6}$ H. $\frac{2}{6}$

   G. $\frac{1}{4}$ J. $\frac{3}{6}$

3. Jean is deciding on an outfit to wear to school. Today, she can choose either a yellow, red, or blue shirt, and either black, blue, or brown pants. How many different combinations of one shirt and one pair of pants can Jean make?

   A. 2   C. 6

   B. 3   D. 9

4. Michelle pulls a single marble from the bag without looking. Which shows the probability that the marble will be black?

   F. $\frac{3}{10}$ H. $\frac{7}{10}$

   G. $\frac{3}{7}$ J. $\frac{7}{7}$

5. Sarah flips a quarter and spins the needle on a spinner that has equal red and black parts. Which shows all the possible outcomes?

   A. heads, black; heads, red; tails, black; tails, red

   B. heads, red; heads, black; tails, red; tails, red

   C. heads, black; tails, black; tails, red

   D. heads, red; heads, black

6. What is the probability that the spinner will land on an even number?

_____

7. A bag holds 6 blue marbles and 4 red marbles. Lisa wants to make the probability of picking out a red marble 1/2. What are two different ways she can do this?

_____

_____

_____

8. Zoe is planning to bake muffins. She will make bran, blueberry, and cornmeal muffins. Then she will top the muffins with walnuts, almonds, or coconut. She makes a tree diagram to show all the possible combinations.

Muffin Type	Topping

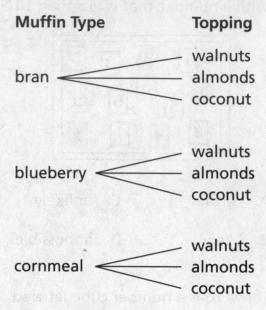

How many possible combinations of one muffin and one topping can Zoe make?

_____

4.2.1 Write and solve equations with (=) to show equivalence and use with variables to express mathematical relationships involving multiplication and division. Plot the points for the corresponding values in the first quadrant.

1. On the first day of her fishing trip Jan caught some fish. On the second day she caught 2 fish. Which expression shows how many fish Jan caught in all?

   A. $f \div 2$ C. $f - 2$

   B. $f + 2$ D. $f \times 2$

2. Mark has 17 drawings. There are some pictures of spaceships, s, and 3 pictures of horses. What symbol best completes this number sentence?

   $$s \square 3 = 17$$

   F. $=$

   G. $+$

   H. $-$

   J. $<$

3. Matteo bought 5 comic books for $12. Each comic book cost the same amount. Which equation shows the price, p, for each comic?

   A. $12 + 5 = p$

   B. $12 \times 5 = p$

   C. $12 - 5 = p$

   D. $12 \div 5 = p$

4. Gina is g years old. She is 7 times older than Val. What expression shows how old Val is?

   F. $g - 7$

   G. $g + 7$

   H. $g \times 7$

   J. $g \div 7$

5. Which equation describes the graph?

   Mika's Workout

   A. $5 + p = w$

   B. $5w = p$

   C. $5 + w = p$

   D. $5p = w$

6. Solve for *n*.

$n \times 8 = 56$

_____

7. Felix did $\frac{1}{5}$ of his math homework at school. Then he did some more before dinner. At dinnertime, Felix had finished $\frac{4}{5}$ of his homework. Write an equation to show how much of his homework Felix completed at home before dinner.

_____

8. Dina is making a rectangular shape out of blocks. One pair of sides is 2 blocks long. The other pair is *x* blocks long. The area of Dina's shape is 20 blocks. Write an equation to show how to find the length of the unknown sides.

x

2

_____

_____

Core Standard 1 Number Sense and Computation

4.2.2 Create, extend, and give a rule for number patterns using multiplication and division and non-numeric growing or repeating patterns.

1. Which equation describes a rule for the table?

Input, x	15	21	33	49	52	65	70
Output, y	27	33	45	61	64	77	82

  A. $x + y = 12$ **C.** $x - 12 = y$

  B. $x + 12 = y$ **D.** $y + 12 = x$

2. Which numbers complete the table?

Input, x	2	4	8	16	32	64	128
Output, y	22	24	28	■	■	■	■

  F. 34, 42, 52, 64   **H.** 36, 52, 84, 148

  G. 22, 40, 74, 140 **J.** 56, 64, 128, 256

3. Which table follows the rule

$a \times 3 = b$?

A.
Input, a	7	9	12	15	23	28	30
Output, b	21	27	36	45	69	84	90

B.
Input, a	7	9	12	15	23	28	30
Output, b	10	12	15	18	26	31	33

C.
Input, a	7	9	12	15	23	28	30
Output, b	21	23	26	29	37	42	44

D.
Input, a	7	9	12	15	23	28	30
Output, b	3	6	9	12	15	18	21

4. Which number pattern shows the rule *subtract 4, multiply by 3*?

  A. 1, 7, 14, 21, 28, 35, 42

  B. 5, 1, 9, 5, 1, 9, 5

  C. 6, 2, 6, 2, 6, 2, 6

  D. 7, 4, 16, 13, 52, 49

5. Miranda is mailing copies of her band's CD to friends.

A package with 8 CDs weighs 2 pounds, a package with 12 CDs weighs 3 pounds, and a package with 16 CDs weighs 4 pounds.

Number of CDs, x	8	12	16
Weight (in pounds), y	2	3	4

Miranda wants to graph the data in her function table.

Show the input/output values as ordered pairs.

_____

57

6. Marcus is raising money for the chess club.

The school has agreed to donate $2 for every $1 that Marcus raises. A game company has also agreed to donate $5 each time someone makes a donation.

Marcus created an input/output table to show how much money the chess club would make for each donation.

Input, s	10	12	19	24	31
Output, t	25	29	43	53	▪

Marcus wrote an equation to show the rule.

$t = (s \times 2) + 5$

Use the rule to complete the table.

What is the missing number?

_____

7. Cory is looking at a map of his hometown. There is a scale at the bottom of the map. It says "1 cm = 1 mile." He measures the distance on the map from his house to his friend Shanice's house. If they are 3 centimeters away from each other on the map, how far apart are their houses in real life?

A. 3 miles

B. 6 miles

C. 9 miles

D. 18 miles

Core Standard 1 Number Sense and Computation

4.2.3 Show that the order in which two numbers are multiplied [commutative property] and how numbers are grouped in multiplication [associative property] will not change the product. Use these properties together to show that numbers can be multiplied in any order.

1. What number makes this number sentence *true*?

$$79 \times 43 = \square \times 79$$

A. 0

B. 1

C. 40

D. 43

2. Which expression is equivalent to $(1{,}945 \times 500) \times 67$?

F. $1{,}945 \times (500 \times 67)$

G. $500 \times (1{,}945 + 67)$

H. $(1{,}945 \times 500) + (1{,}945 \times 67)$

J. $(5 \times 1{,}945 \times 67) +$
   $(100 \times 1{,}945 \times 67)$

3. What is the missing number in this expression?

$$5 \times 4 \times 8 = 4 \times \underline{\quad} \times 5$$

A. 4   C. 8

B. 5   D. 20

4. What is the missing number? What property of multiplication does this number sentence show?

$$14 \times (7 \times 9) = \square \times (9 \times 14)$$

_____

5. Evaluate given $n = 4$.

$$(5 \times 2) \times (10 \times n)$$

A. 400

B. 100

C. 40

D. 20

6. Which property of multiplication does this number sentence show?

$$32 \times 12 = 12 \times 32$$

_____

7. In the downtown parking lot there were 5 rows of cars with 12 cars in each row. The manager of the lot rearranged the cars so that there were 12 rows of cars. Write an expression to show how you can find out how many cars are in each row. Tell what property you used and solve.

_____

_____

_____

8. Mr. Gray has 12 boxes of crayons with 8 crayons in a box. He wants to divide the crayons equally among 8 students. How many crayons will each student receive?

_____

Getting Ready for the ISTEP+

4.2.4 **Use the distributive property in expressions involving multiplication.**

1. Which expression correctly uses the distributive property to find the product 7 × 19?

   A. (7 × 10) + (19 × 10)

   B. (4 × 19) + (3 × 19)

   C. (4 × 19) − (3 × 19)

   D. (4 × 10) + (3 × 10) + (19 × 10)

2. Supply the missing number to find the product 32 × 225.

   (□ × 225) + (2 × 225)

   F. 3

   G. 2

   H. 30

   J. 32

3. What expression is modeled by the array model?

   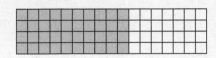

   A. 17 × 4 = (10 × 4) + (17 × 4)

   B. 17 × 4 = (10 × 7) + (4 × 7)

   C. 17 × 4 = (10 × 17) + (17 × 4)

   D. 17 × 4 = (10 × 4) + (7 × 4)

4. Reyna wants to use the distributive property to solve this expression.

   40 × 117

   Which expression should Reyna use?

   F. (40 × 100) × (40 × 10) × (40 × 7)

   G. (40 × 100) + (40 × 10) + (40 × 7)

   H. (40 + 100) × (40 + 10) × (40 + 7)

   J. (40 + 100) + (40 + 10) + (40 + 7

5. Mark needs to solve this equation.

   20 × 359 = □

   Which expression can Mark use to find the product?

   A. (20 × 3) + (20 × 5) + (20 × 9)

   B. (20 × 3) + (20 × 100) + (20 × 59)

   C. (20 × 300) + (20 × 50) + (20 × 9)

   D. (20 + 300) + (20 + 50) + (20 + 9)

6. Find the missing number. Then write *commutative, associative,* or *distributive* to name the property you used.

   24 × 38 = (24 × □) + (24 × 8)

   _____

7. Write an expression using the distributive property to represent the array model.

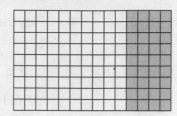

_____

8. Explain how you can use the distributive property to find the product of 6 and 37.

_____

_____

_____

Core Standard 2 Geometry and Measurement

4.3.1 Identify, describe and draw pairs of parallel lines, perpendicular lines, and nonperpendicular intersecting lines using appropriate mathematical tools and technology.

1. Which shows a line segment?

A.

B.

C.

D. •

2. Victor drew this figure in his notebook.

What is the best name for Victor's figure?

F. angle

G. line

H. line segment

J. ray

3. Brett drew these 4 sets of lines using her computer. Which set of lines is not parallel?

A.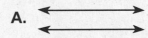

B.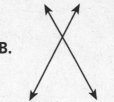

C.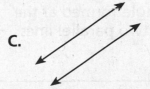

D.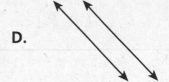

4. Which street on the map appears to be parallel to Mulberry Street?

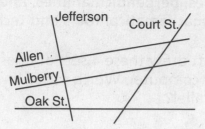

F. Oak Street

G. Court Street

H. Jefferson Street

J. Allen Street

5. Describe the angle formed at the intersection of two parallel lines.

_____

_____

_____

6. Adam drew these lines.

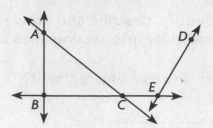

Which line appears to be perpendicular to $\overleftrightarrow{BE}$?

_____

Core Standard 2 Geometry and Measurement

4.3.2 Identify, describe and draw right angles, acute angles, obtuse angles, straight angles and rays using appropriate tools and technology.

1. Which is an angle less than 90°?

    A. right angle

    B. obtuse angle

    C. acute angle

    D. straight angle

2. Which triangle contains a right angle?

     F.

     G.

    H.

     J.

3. How many obtuse angles can a rectangle have?

    A. 4

    B. 3

    C. 2

    D. 0

4. Which best describes the angles in a parallelogram that is not a rectangle?

    A. There are two right angles and two acute angles.

    B. There are four right angles.

    C. There are four acute angles.

    D. There are two acute angles and two obtuse angles.

5. How does a straight angle compare with a right angle?

_____

_____

_____

_____

6. Look at the regular pentagon.

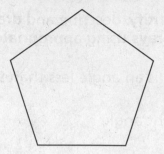

Describe the angles of this figure.

_____

_____

Name _____

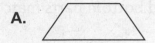 **4.3.3** **Identify shapes that have reflectional and rotational symmetry.**

1. Which figure does not have rotational symmetry?

A.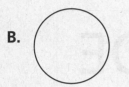

B.

C.

D.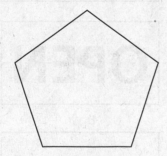

2. The figure below has rotational symmetry.

During one full turn, how many times will the figure match its original position?

F. 2   H. 4

G. 3   J. 5

3. Which figure has reflectional symmetry?

A.

B.

C.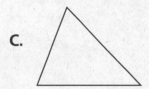

D.

Name _____

Name _____

4. Alicia drew a line on each of the four equilateral triangles. Which triangle shows a line of symmetry?

F.

H.

G.

J.

5. Which letters in the word below have reflectional symmetry?

SHAVE

A. V, E

B. S, A

C. H, A, V

D. S, V, E

6. Oscar is making flashcards for a vocabulary game. Each card has 1 word printed on it.

Oscar wants to find words that have a line of symmetry so that when the words are folded along a horizontal line the top and bottom parts match exactly.

This is the first flashcard he makes.

Which shows another word that has a similar line of symmetry?

F.

G.

H.

J.

4.3.4 Measure and draw line segments to the nearest eighth-inch and millimeter.

1. How long is the line shown to the nearest $\frac{1}{8}$ inch?

_____

A. $3\frac{2}{8}$ inches   B. $4\frac{3}{8}$ inches

C. $4\frac{4}{8}$ inches   D. $4\frac{5}{8}$ inches

2. Use an inch ruler. What is the length of the drawing of the cherry to the nearest eighth inch?

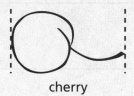

cherry

F. $1\frac{3}{8}$ inches   G. $1\frac{2}{8}$ inches

H. $2\frac{3}{8}$ inches   J. $2\frac{2}{8}$ inches

3. Use a millimeter ruler. What is the length of the battery to the nearest millimeter?

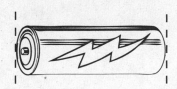

A. 36 millimeters   B. 44 millimeters

C. 40 millimeters   D. 50 millimeters

4. Use your ruler. How long is the drawing of the feather, to the nearest millimeter?

F. 45 millimeters

G. 55 millimeters

H. 65 millimeters

J. 75 millimeters

5. How long is the line shown to the nearest centimeter?

_____

A. 3 centimeters

B. 4 centimeters

C. 5 centimeters

D. 6 centimeters

6. Use a millimeter ruler. Find the length of one long side and one short side of the rectangle.

Long side_____

Short side _____

7. Use an inch ruler and a millimeter ruler to measure this drawing of a paper clip.

What is the length of the paper clip in inches?

_____

About how many millimeters long is the paper clip?

_____

_____

Core Standard 2 Geometry and Measurement

 4.3.5 Develop and use formulas for finding the perimeter and area of rectangles, including squares, using appropriate strategies (e.g. decomposing shapes), tools and units of measure.

1. What is the formula for finding the area of a rectangle l inches long and w inches wide?

   A. $l^2 + w^2$

   B. $2l + 2w$

   C. $(l + w)^2$

   D. $l \times w$

2. What is the area of the square figure below?

   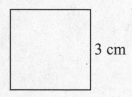
   3 cm

   F. 3 cm^2 H. 6 cm^2

   G. 9 cm^2 J. 12 cm^2

3. What is the perimeter of the rectangle below?

   2 feet
   6 feet

   A. 16 ft   C. 12 ft

   B. 10 ft   D. 8 ft

4. How can you find the area of the rectangle shown below?

   F. Add $9 + 3$ H. Subtract 3 from 9

   G. Multiply 9×3 J. Divide 9 by 3

5. Compare the perimeter of a square 4 cm on a side with the perimeter of a rectangle 8 cm long and 2 cm wide.

   A. The perimeters of the square and the rectangle are equal.

   B. The perimeter of the rectangle is greater by 4 cm.

   C. The perimeter of the square is greater by 4 cm.

   D. The perimeter of the rectangle is 4 cm less.

6. Find the area of the square below.

   7 inches

7. Use the formula $P = 2(l + w)$ to find the perimeter of the rectangle below.

Show your work.

8. Find the perimeter and area of the figure below.

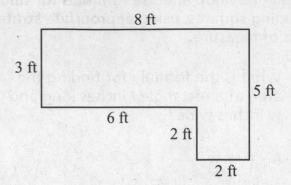

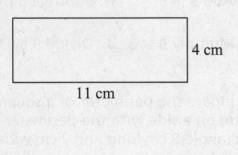

_____

_____

_____

_____

Name _____

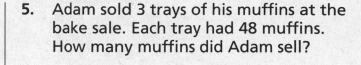

Multiply and Divide 2-Digit by 1-Digit

1. There are 5 fourth-grade classes going to the zoo. Each class has 25 students. How many students are going to the zoo?

   _____

2. What is the product?

   $$\begin{array}{r} 89 \\ \times\ 2 \\ \hline \end{array}$$

   _____

3. Jack types 32 words per minute. How many words can he type in 8 minutes?

   $$\begin{array}{r} 32 \\ \times\ 8 \\ \hline \end{array}$$

   _____

4. What is 45 × 9?

   _____

5. Adam sold 3 trays of his muffins at the bake sale. Each tray had 48 muffins. How many muffins did Adam sell?

   _____

6. What is the product?

   $$\begin{array}{r} 79 \\ \times\ 4 \\ \hline \end{array}$$

   _____

7. There are 20 ounces of juice in one bottle. How many ounces are in 6 bottles?

   _____

8. What is 57 × 3?

   _____

9. What is the quotient?

$3\overline{)96}$

_____

10. What is 52 ÷ 2?

_____

11. Kimya has 75 beads to make bracelets. She uses the same number of beads for each of 3 bracelets. How many beads does she use for each bracelet?

_____

12. What is the quotient?

$5\overline{)95}$

_____

13. Mrs. Ishi drives 88 miles in 2 days. She drives the same number of miles each day. How many miles does she drive each day?

_____

14. What is 84 ÷ 4?

_____

15. There are 3 rows of cabbage on Mr. Rex's farm. There are a total of 72 cabbages. How many cabbages are in each row?

_____

16. What is 60 ÷ 4?

_____

Parallel and Perpendicular Lines

1. Are the lines shown below parallel, perpendicular, or non-perpendicular intersecting?

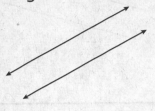

_____

2. Are the lines shown below parallel, perpendicular, or non-perpendicular intersecting?

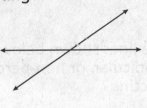

_____

_____

3. Describe non-perpendicular intersecting lines.

_____

_____

_____

_____

4. Are the lines shown below parallel, perpendicular, or non-perpendicular intersecting?

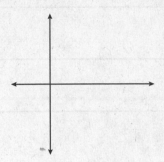

_____

5. Describe parallel lines.

_____

_____

_____

_____

6. Draw a pair of non-perpendicular intersecting lines.

_____

Name _____

7. Describe perpendicular lines.

    _____

    _____

    _____

    _____

8. Are the lines shown below parallel,
    perpendicular, or non-perpendicular
    intersecting?

    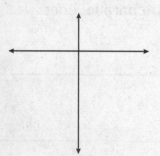

    _____

9. Draw a pair of perpendicular
    intersecting lines.

    _____

10. Are the lines shown below parallel,
    perpendicular, or non-perpendicular
    intersecting?

    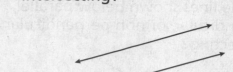

    _____

11. Draw a pair of parallel lines.

    _____

12. Are the lines shown below parallel,
    perpendicular, or non-perpendicular
    intersecting?

    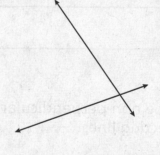

    _____

    _____

Lines and Angles

1. Is the angle shown below an acute angle, a right angle, an obtuse angle, or a straight angle?

_____

2. Draw a right angle.

_____

3. Describe an acute angle.

_____

_____

_____

4. Is the angle shown below an acute angle, a right angle, an obtuse angle, or a straight angle?

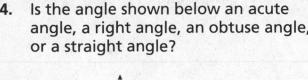

5. Draw a ray.

_____

6. Is the angle shown below an acute angle, a right angle, an obtuse angle, or a straight angle?

_____

7. Draw an obtuse angle.

_____

8. Describe a straight angle.

_____

_____

9. Is the angle shown below an acute angle, a right angle, an obtuse angle, or a straight angle?

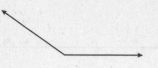

_____

10. Is the angle shown below an acute angle, a right angle, an obtuse angle, or a straight angle?

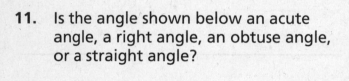

_____

11. Is the angle shown below an acute angle, a right angle, an obtuse angle, or a straight angle?

_____

12. Draw a straight angle.

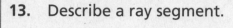

_____

13. Describe a ray segment.

_____

_____

_____

14. Describe an obtuse angle.

_____

_____

_____

_____

15. Draw a right angle.

_____

Compare and Order Fractions

1. The fraction bars below show $\frac{3}{8}$ and $\frac{2}{4}$.

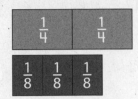

Compare $\frac{3}{8}$ and $\frac{2}{4}$ using $<$, $>$, or $=$.

_____

2. Mahmet owns $\frac{3}{4}$ pounds of silver. Derya owns $\frac{6}{8}$ pounds of gold. Use the fraction bars below to compare the fractions. Use $<$, $>$, or $=$.

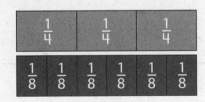

_____

3. Alberto owns a collection of model cars. $\frac{2}{5}$ of his model cars are red, and $\frac{3}{10}$ of his model cars are black. The number lines below show the fractions.

Compare $\frac{2}{5}$ and $\frac{3}{10}$ using $<$, $>$, or $=$.

_____

4. Use the benchmark fractions 0, $\frac{1}{2}$, or 1 to compare $\frac{4}{5}$ and $\frac{3}{6}$. Use the symbols $<$, $>$, or $=$.

Name _____

5. A recipe calls for $\frac{5}{6}$ cup of brown sugar. Which benchmark fraction is the fraction closest to: 0, $\frac{1}{2}$, or 1?

_____

6. Of the students in Edwina's class, $\frac{1}{2}$ have brown hair and $\frac{2}{5}$ have blond hair. The fraction models below show these fractions.

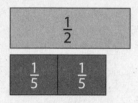

Compare $\frac{1}{2}$ and $\frac{2}{5}$ using the symbols <, >, or =.

_____

7. Of Jemma's friends, $\frac{2}{10}$ say that orange is their favorite color. Which benchmark is the fraction closest to: 0, $\frac{1}{2}$, or 1?

_____

8. Antonio found out that $\frac{3}{5}$ of his friends own a cat or a dog. Which benchmark fraction is the fraction closest to: 0, $\frac{1}{2}$, or 1?

_____

9. Anna ran $\frac{4}{5}$ of a mile. Bob ran $\frac{5}{6}$ of a mile. Use the number line to compare the distances they ran. Use <, >, or =.

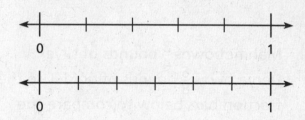

_____

10. Use the benchmarks 0, $\frac{1}{2}$, or 1 to compare $\frac{6}{10}$ and $\frac{2}{8}$. Use the symbols <, >, or =.

_____

Getting Ready for the ISTEP+

Perimeter and Area of Rectangles

1. Find the perimeter of the following shape.

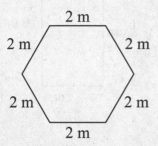

2. Find the area of a 7 inch by 7 inch square.

_____

3. Find the perimeter of the following shape.

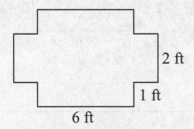

4. Find the area of the following shape.

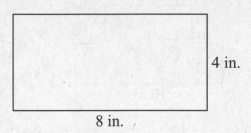

5. Find the perimeter of the following shape.

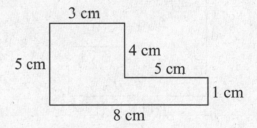

6. Find the area of a 6 meter by 9 meter rectangle.

_____

7. Find the perimeter of the following figure.

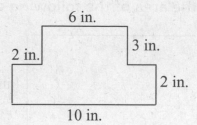

_____

8. Find the perimeter of the following figure.

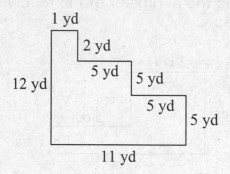

_____

9. Find the area of a 27 foot by 32 foot rectangular garden.

_____

10. Find the area of the following figure.

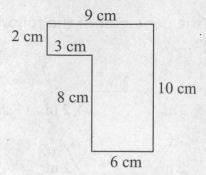

_____

11. Find the perimeter of the following figure.

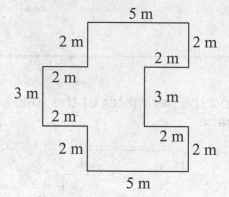

_____

12. Find the perimeter of a $4\frac{1}{2}$ inch by $4\frac{1}{2}$ inch square.

_____

NCAA Hall of Champions

The NCAA (National Collegiate Athletic Association) began in 1910 with the first national championship being held in 1921 (the National Collegiate Track and Field Championships). The NCAA Hall of Champions, located in Indianapolis, Indiana, first opened in March 2000. A new facility opened in March of 2009 after closing in November of 2007 due to a fire. The current facility is dedicated to the education of student athletes through interactive exhibitions and events.

1. The current NCAA Hall of Champions is a 30,000 square foot facility made up of various exhibitions and meeting spaces. The Great Hall is the 4,200 square foot entryway. It welcomes people with three stories of glass and light. Write the number 4,200 in expanded form.

   _____

2. The Hall of Honor celebrates the achievements of current and former student athletes. The Hall also exhibits photos of people who have received the NCAA's highest honors and awards. The Hall of Honor is 470 square feet. Plot the number 470 on a number line labeled in increments of 50.

3. The Member Showcase pays tribute to member institutions from the viewpoint of the NCAA student athletes. The Member Showcase is two thousand two hundred square feet. Write this number in standard form and in expanded form.

   _____

4. The NCAA Hall of Champions currently offers two meeting spaces. Champion Hall is 3,200 square feet featuring the NCAA magazine, Champion. The Gallery is smaller at 2,200 square feet. It is also sometimes used for temporary or traveling exhibits. Plot the numbers 3,200 and 2,200 on a number line labeled in increments of 200. Then use <, >, or = to compare the areas of the two meeting spaces.

   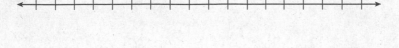

   _____

The National Collegiate Athletic Association (NCAA) is an organization through which the nation's colleges and universities govern their athletics programs. It is made up of colleges and universities, conferences, organizations, and individuals committed to the education and athletic participation of student athletes.

5. In 2008, Vanderbilt was the leader in batting averages with 0.389. Florida State followed with a batting average of 0.380. Place 0.389 and 0.380 on a number line marked in hundredths.

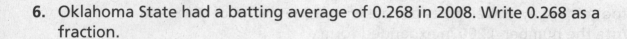

6. Oklahoma State had a batting average of 0.268 in 2008. Write 0.268 as a fraction.

_____

7. Texas University had an ERA (earned run average) of 3.5 in 2008. Model 3.5 on the grids below.

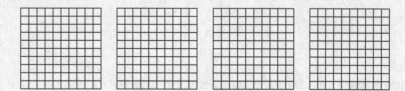

8. In 2008, Arizona State had a batting average of 0.366. Is 0.366 closer to 0 or to 1?

_____

Indianapolis Motor Speedway Hall of Fame

The Indianapolis Motor Speedway Hall of Fame Museum is located northwest of Indianapolis on the grounds of the Indianapolis Motor Speedway. The original Hall of Fame opened in 1956. A larger museum was built in 1975 within the Speedway oval.

1. The Tony Hulman Theater at the Indianapolis Motor Speedway Hall of Fame features a 20-minute presentation of rare historic footage and Indianapolis 500 highlights. The theater has 48 seats. If there are 5 showings a day and the theater is full for each, how many people are watching the 20-minute presentation each day?

_____

2. If each visual presentation is only half full, how many people are watching the presentation in a week (7 days)?

_____

3. If the Tony Hulman Theater is open 7 days a week and there are 12 daily showings of the 20-minute presentation, how many minutes each week is the visual presentation being shown?

_____

4. The museum is open 364 days a year from 9 A.M. to 5 P.M. How many hours in a year is the museum open?

_____

5. Admission to the museum is $3 for adults and $1 for children ages 6-15. A middle school group consisting of 14 teachers and 70 students visits the museum. Write and solve an equation to find out how much the group will have to pay for admissions, n.

_____

The Indianapolis Motor Speedway is home to the famous Indianapolis 500-mile race held every May. The annual event brings thousands of spectators to Indianapolis every year.

6. The tread depth of an IndyCar Series tire is $\frac{3}{32}$ of an inch, which is slightly thicker than a credit card. Find three equivalent fractions for $\frac{3}{32}$.

_____

7. At speeds of 220 mph (miles per hour), the front tires of an IndyCar Series car rotate at a rate of 43 times per second. How many times per second will the front tires of IndyCar Series car rotate in one minute (60 seconds)?

_____

8. The oval track at the Indianapolis Motor Speedway is 2.5 miles long. Write this decimal as a fraction.

_____

9. Display the following ages of people who went to the Indianapolis 500 from your local youth group: 15, 12, 12, 13, 16, 8, 11, 17, 16, 13, 12, 10, 9, 15, 10 as a line plot. Identify the median, range, and mode of the data.

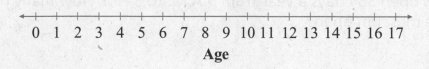

Age

_____

Black Pine Animal Park

Black Pine Animal Park in Albion, Indiana, was founded in
1995. It is an exotic animal sanctuary for rescued and retired
animals. The park is home to over 70 big and small cats,
bears, primates, birds, reptiles, and other former pets and
performers.

1. "Mona Lisa," also called "Lisa", is a lion-tailed macaques
   who used to be a pet. If Lisa's habitat at the Park is 90
   yards by 90 yards, what is the area and perimeter of Lisa's
   habitat?

   _____

   _____

2. Black Pine Animal Park is currently home to six Bengal tigers: Montrose,
   Cita, Jai, Darly, Luna, and India. The length of the head and body of Bengal
   tigers is usually 5 feet to 6 feet. The length of their tails is usually 2 to 3
   feet. If the length of a tiger's head and body is $5\frac{1}{4}$ feet and the length of its
   tail is $5\frac{1}{4}$ feet, how long is the tiger from head to tail? Draw pattern blocks
   or fraction bars to find the answer.

   _____

3. Mr. Bear and Isaac are former circus bears enjoying retirement at Black Pine
   Animal Park. Bears can run up to 30 mph (miles per hour). If a bear runs for
   a total of 2 hours a day at 30 mph, how far does the bear run in 5 days?

   _____

4. As of 2009, there are five types of primates at the Black Pine Animal Park: baboons, chimpanzees, greater bush babies, lion-tailed macaques, and rhesus macaque monkeys. You only have time to see two of the primates. List all the possible combinations of primates you can visit.

_____

_____

_____

_____

_____

_____

_____

_____

5. You can only visit two of the following four exhibits: African lion, chimpanzees, black bear, and llamas. List all the possible combinations you can visit.

_____

_____

_____

_____

_____

_____

Bluesprings Caverns

Bluesprings Caverns, located in Bedford, Indiana, gives mile-long guided tours of a subterranean river. Along the tour, guides point out native rare blind fish and crayfish while explaining how the caverns were created over time and still, to this day, continue to be shaped by water and time.

1. Custom boats were made for touring the caverns. These boats have on-board lighting, since the caverns are in complete darkness. If these custom boats are a rectangular shape with a length of 12 feet and a width of 5 feet, what is the area and perimeter of these boats?

_____

_____

2. Display the following ages of one group of people visiting the caverns: 6, 24, 16, 12, 30, 10, 32, 7, 30, 14, 10, 35, 8, 10, 40 as a line plot. Identify the median, range, and mode of your data.

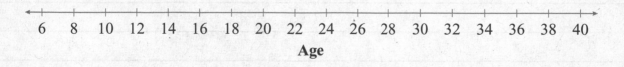

Age

Bluesprings Caverns' "Overnight Adventure" program is a unique winter camping experience one hundred feet underground designed for youth groups ages 9 to 16. Groups are able to explore the underground river first by boat. Then they walk, crawl, and climb in undeveloped areas which are not seen on the regular tour. Groups then camp overnight in Canyon Hall above the Myst'ry River.

3. Display the following ages of one group of people participating in the overnight adventure: 12, 16, 22, 15, 25, 12, 10, 13, 15, 11, 14, 12, 24, 27, 13, 11, 10, 15, 16, 14 as a line plot. Identify the median, range, and mode of your data.

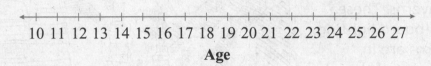

10 11 12 13 14 15 16 17 18 19 20 21 22 23 24 25 26 27

Age

_____

4. The minimum group size is 15 people with 90 being the maximum number. If the cost for each person is $25, how much would the group above have to pay

_____

5. At the "Cave Inn" snack bar, there is a choice of three types of sandwiches: turkey, ham, and roast beef. There are also three types of cheese available: American, Swiss, and provolone. List all the possible combinations of sandwich meet and cheese.

_____
_____
_____
_____
_____
_____
_____
_____
_____

Markland Locks and Dam

The Markland Locks and Dam is a concrete dam that spans the Ohio River connecting Switzerland County, Indiana and Gallatin County, Kentucky.

1. The height of the gates in the dam are 42 feet. The width of these gates is 100 feet. Find the area and perimeter of the gates in the Markland Locks and Dam.

_____

_____

_____

_____

2. The sketch below represents one of the gates in the Markland Dam. Identify a pair of parallel lines and a pair of perpendicular lines.

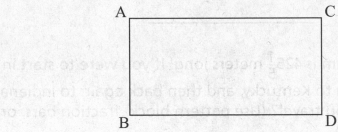

_____

_____

3. If there are twelve gates in the dam, what is the total perimeter and area of all the gates combined?

_____

_____

The Markland Locks and Dam is located on the Ohio River $3\frac{1}{2}$ miles downstream from Warsaw, Kentucky and $26\frac{1}{2}$ miles upstream from Madison, Indiana. The dam is also $531\frac{1}{2}$ miles below Pittsburgh, Pennsylvania.

4. What is the distance from Warsaw, Kentucky to Madison, Indiana?

_____

5. From 2000 to 2005, Markland Locks and Dam processed an average of 51.8 million tons of waterborne commerce each year. Place 51.8 on a number line marked in tenths.

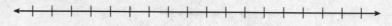

_____

6. The upper pool above the Markland Locks and Dam extends upstream 95.3 miles to the Meldahl Locks and Dam. Write 95.3 as a fraction.

_____

7. The Markland Locks and Dam is $425\frac{1}{5}$ meters long. If you were to start in Indiana, run across the dam to Kentucky, and then back again to Indiana, how many meters would you travel? (Use pattern block, fraction bars, or some other model to solve.)

_____

The Little 500

The Little 500 began in 1950 as a way to raise scholarship money for students working their way through school. This bicycle race has become the largest intramural event on the Indiana University Bloomington campus and the largest collegiate bike race in the United States.

1. Four-person teams compete around a quarter-mile track. Team members exchange bicycles from one teammate to another to complete the race in the least amount of time. There are separate races for men and women. If there are three female teams competing in one race, list all the possible outcomes of the race.

_____

_____

_____

_____

_____

2. If there are 15 races in a day and each race has 6 teams that are participating, how many teams are riding in one day?

_____

3. Display the following ages of some of the participating men's team members: 18, 20, 22, 19, 18, 23, 20, 20, 25, 19, 18, 24, 20, 22, 21, 21, 20, 26, 22, 22. Identify the median, range, and mode of the data.

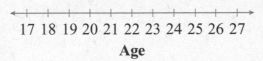

17 18 19 20 21 22 23 24 25 26 27
Age

_____

The Little Fifty is the runner's version of the Little 500. Any Indiana University Bloomington undergraduate who is not a varsity runner may compete. The Little Fifty is a fifty-lap relay competition. Individual men's and women's races are held consisting of twenty-five teams of four students each. The event helps provide scholarships for working students.

4. How many total teams compete in the Little Fifty?

   _____

5. How many total people participate in the Little Fifty?

   _____

6. The Mini 500 Trike Race preceded the Little Fifty. It was established in 1955 as a way for women to participate in the Little 500 race, which at the time was male only. This was a two-lap race on custom-made tricycles having larger front wheels and stronger frames. Teams were made up of four people and an optional coach. Find the number n that satisfies the equation $n \times 4 = 20$, where n represents the number of four-person teams competing.

   _____

Number and Operations

Unscramble the letters to make a word that matches the definition.

1. T I D I G

_____

any one of the ten symbols 0, 1, 2, 3, 4, 5, 6, 7, 8, 9 used to write numbers

2. L A Q I E N E V U T

_____

having the same value

3. R E M O T U N A R

_____

the number above the bar in a fraction, which tells how many parts of the whole are being counted

4. D N R U O

_____

to replace a number with another number that tells about how many or about how much

5. T Q O I N U E T

_____

the number, not including the remainder, that results from dividing

6. M E L I C A D

_____

a number with one or more digits to the right of the decimal point

Name _____

Vocabulary Practice

Write the word that best completes the definition.

1. _____ is a way to write numbers by showing the value of each digit. For example, 397 = 300 + 90 + 7. (expanded form, word form, standard form)

2. A number that is multiplied by another to find a product is called a _____. (multiple, product, factor)

3. A number that names part of a whole or part of a group is called a _____. (fraction, remainder, benchmark number)

4. An amount given as a whole number and a fraction is a _____. (decimal, mixed number, benchmark number)

5. The amount left over when a number cannot be divided equally is called the _____. (dividend, quotient, remainder)

6. Two or more fractions that name the same amount are called _____ fractions. (equivalent, unlike, improper)

7. The number that is to be divided in a division problem is called the _____. (dividend, divisor, quotient)

8. The product of two counting numbers is a _____ of those numbers. (compound, multiple, factor)

Algebra

Write the value of each variable.

1. $(6 + 3) + 2 = a + (3 + 2)$

_____

2. $b + 0 = 3$

_____

3. $6 \times 8 = 8 \times c$

_____

4. $9 \times a = 0$

_____

5. $3 + 7 = b + 3$

_____

6. $c \times 1 = 6$

_____

7. $(5 \times 9) \times 3 = 5 \times (a \times 3)$

_____

8. $7 \times (5 + 6) = (b \times 5) + (7 \times 6)$

_____

Use the definitions below to complete the puzzle.

Across

4. a part of a number sentence that has numbers and operation signs but does not have an equal sign

5. a number sentence which shows that two quantities are equal

6. a table that matches each input value with an output value (2 words)

Down

1. operations that undo each other (2 words)

2. a special set of rules that gives the order in which calculations are done in an expression (3 words)

3. a letter or symbol that stands for a number or numbers

Geometry

Complete the chart.

Figure	Name	Number of Sides	Number of Angles	Number of Vertices

Name _____

Use the definitions below to complete the puzzle.

Across

2. a word describing two lines that intersect to form four right angles

4. a polygon with six sides and six angles

6. a closed figure made up of points that are the same distance from the center

Down

1. a grid formed by a horizontal line called the x-axis and a vertical line called the y-axis (2 words)

3. a pair of numbers used to locate a point on a coordinate grid (2 words)

5. a straight path of points on a plane that continues without end in both directions with no endpoints

7. an exact location in space

 Getting Ready for the ISTEP+

Measurement

Circle the best word to complete each sentence.

1. To measure your height, you would use (kilometers, inches).

2. If you were to fill a bathtub, you would need about 30 (cups, gallons).

3. A football field is 100 (yards, feet) long.

4. The time it takes someone to run one mile would be measured in (seconds, minutes).

5. A centimeter ruler is used to find the (length weight) of a pencil.

6. The size of an angle is measured in (degrees, inches).

7. To find her (height, weight), Shana uses a scale.

8. Jules uses a measuring cup to find the (height, capacity) of a water pitcher.

9. Meridith is building a fence around her garden. She needs to find the (length, capacity) of each side.

10. In order to know how much a container can hold you would have to find its (weight, capacity).

11. The perimeter of Mr. Danson's backyard is 160 (feet square feet).

12. Thirty-six inches is the same as one (foot, yard).

Name _____

Write the term that matches each example.

digital clock	centimeters
pounds	minutes
feet	seconds
analog clock	inches

1.

   The time on this _____ is 12:30.

2.

   The time on this _____ is 7:45.

3. A German Shepherd dog is weighed on a scale that says the dog

   weighs 145 _____.

4. Connor measures his finger, and finds that it

   measures 7 _____.

5. There are 60 _____ in a minute

   and 60 _____ in an hour.

6. There are 12 _____ in a foot and

   3 _____ in a yard.

Data Analysis and Probability

Use the following graph and the terms in the box below to complete the sentences.

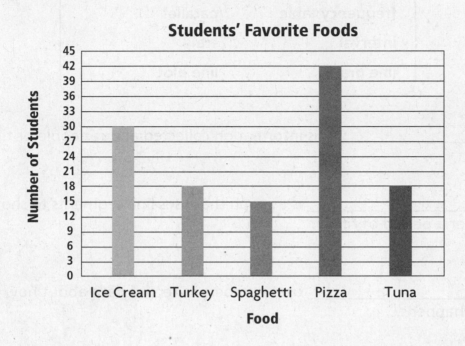

Students' Favorite Foods

1. This type of graph is called a _____.

2. The _____ of this graph is found by subtracting the lowest number from the highest number.

3. The _____, or the number most repeated, of the data on this graph is 18.

4. The _____ of this graph is 3.

5. To find the _____, you would arrange the data in order and find the middle value.

6. The data for this graph was collected from students who took a _____.

mode

median

bar graph

survey

interval

range

Name _____

Use the words in the Word Bank to complete each statement.

```
                    Word Bank
    data                perpendicular
    frequency table     parallel
    interval            scale
    line graph          line plot
```

1. _____ is information collected about people or things.

2. A _____ is a graph that uses line segments to show how data changes over a period of time.

3. A _____ uses numbers to record data about how often something happens.

4. Lines that intersect to form right angles are _____ lines.

5. The _____ of a graph is a series of numbers starting at zero and place at fixed distances to label the graph.

6. The _____ is the distance between two numbers on the scale of a number line.

7. A _____ is a number line with marks or dots that shows frequency.

8. Lines in a plane that do not intersect are _____ lines.

Inch/Centimeter Ruler

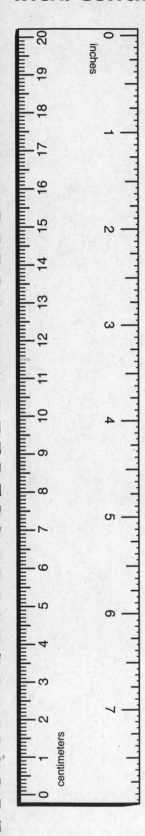